Christmas Crossroads

30 Devotionals for the
Holiday Season

Jean Wise

Copyright © 2018 by Jean Wise.
ISBN 978-0-9992502-0-4

All rights reserved. No part of this publication may be reproduced, distributed, or transmitted in any form or by any means, including photocopying, recording, or other electronic or mechanical methods, without the prior written permission of the publisher, except in the case of brief quotations embodied in critical reviews and certain other noncommercial uses permitted by copyright law. For permission requests, write to the publisher, addressed "Attention: Permissions Coordinator," at the address below.

Healthy Spirituality Publishing
Edon Ohio
www.healthyspirituality.org

All Scripture quotations, unless otherwise indicated, are taken from the Holy Bible, New International Version®, NIV®.
Copyright ©1973, 1978, 1984, 2011 by Biblica, Inc.™ Used by permission of Zondervan. All rights reserved worldwide. www.zondervan.com The "NIV" and "New
International Version" are trademarks registered in the United States Patent and Trademark Office by Biblica, Inc.

Scripture quotations marked MSG are taken from THE MESSAGE, copyright © 1993, 1994, 1995, 1996, 2000, 2001, 2002 by Eugene H. Peterson. Used by permission of NavPress. All rights reserved. Represented by Tyndale House Publishers, Inc.

Scripture quotations marked (NLT) are taken from the Holy Bible, New Living Translation, copyright ©1996, 2004, 2015 by Tyndale House Foundation. Used by permission of Tyndale House Publishers, Inc., Carol Stream, Illinois 60188. All rights reserved.

Christmas Crossroads Bonus!

Interested in learning more about Advent?

Click here to receive a free Advent Resource Guide:

http://healthyspirituality.org/advent

Thank you!

Introduction

How do we decide which way to turn in the all the crossroads of life?
The crazy chaos of the holiday season descends upon our souls quickly, complicating our journey. We crave the peace, joy, and hope during Advent, but often we only experience uproar and mayhem.
The intersection of uncertain choices merged with the holidays compounds our decisions.

Christmas Crossroads - 30 Devotionals for the Holiday Season will enrich your time before Christmas, prepare your heart for celebrating the birth of Christ, and lead you to a clearer understanding of discernment in the crossroads of life.

Christmas Crossroads - 30 Devotionals for the Holiday Season will help you to:
- Approach Christmas with an open and receiving heart.
- Explore making the best choices at the crossroads encounter in life.
- Listen to people of the Bible and gather inspiration and guidance from their crossroad experience.
- Apply new ways to make the right decisions on our life journey.
- Grow closer to God in quiet reflections as you seek God's guidance during the holidays.

A Prayer for your Journey

My Lord God,
I have no idea where I am going.
I do not see the road ahead of me.

I cannot know for certain where it will end.
Nor do I really know myself,
and the fact that I think that I am following
your will does not mean that I am actually doing so.
But I believe that the desire to please you does in fact please you.

And I hope I have that desire in all that I am doing.
I hope that I will never do anything apart from that desire.
And I know that if I do this, you will lead me by the right road
though I may know nothing about it.

Therefore will I trust you always though I may seem to be lost and in
the shadow of death. I will not fear, for you are ever with me,
and you will never leave me to face my perils alone.

Amen.

Thomas Merton

Roads in our Life Journey

The Crossroads of our Life

This is what the Lord says:
"Stand at the crossroads and look; ask for the ancient paths, ask where the good way is, and walk in it, and you will find rest for your souls."
Jeremiah 6: 16

Pause for a moment and think about the roads in your life. The street where your childhood home dwelled. The neighborhood surrounding your school. The route you drove or still drive to work. Your favorite avenue to shop. A path you enjoy for a walk. The vacation spot that brings you joy.

Our whole life can also be envisioned as a winding, unpredictable, wildly enchanting, yet frightening, unknown journey. Everyone's walk arrives at intersections where we must decide to keep going straight or make a change. Sometimes we can choose our direction; other times the decision is out of our control. Our lifepath twists and turns like a turbulent roller coaster, no matter how carefully planned or imagined.

Consider the crossroads you have already experienced. Where to attend school? Whom to marry? Which job to take? What lessons did you learn from those times?

The crazy chaos of the holiday season is quickly coming, and this time of year complicates our journey. We crave peace, joy, and hope in this time of year, but often only experience uproar and mayhem.

Perhaps you are approaching a new crossroads. The intersection of uncertain choices merged with the holiday compounds the decision, and our next steps waver.

As I write these devotions, I am anticipating a major change in my routines and my "well planned" schedule with increasing demands on my time. I am unsure what to let go or which way to turn. I pray for direction as I turn to scripture.

The wisdom from these words in today's verse soothes my anxious soul. I don't see in these verses any notation of fear, apprehension, or concern. The word rest resonates in my heart.

In these verses from Jeremiah, we are encouraged to stand at those crossroads and look, ask, then walk.

Sometimes our best move is to stand still and look. Pay attention to what God is telling us in this present moment. Advent is a wonderful opportunity to listen to God, knowing his wisdom will emerge and guide us onward in whatever direction we take.

Crossroad discernment takes time. Listen to the wisdom from Jeremiah when you face decisions: Stand and look. Many intersections have stop lights or stop signs for a reason. Our safety is one reason, but these can be moments to stop at these points in our lives and look around. What do we see? Hear? Allow time to rest before proceeding into the next season.

Ask for guidance before walking forward. God will provide direction for our next steps.
Then we walk forward, knowing God is with us and we are heading on the right path.

We approach Christmas in the same way. Hit the pause button for a moment and look at the riches and meaning of Jesus' birth. Listen for the lessons God is showing us in this sacred season.

Walk, don't run, through the holiday. Savor the time of stopping for God moments

God will reveal the light for our next steps just as he revealed the Light for all at Bethlehem.

Roadside Billboard:

One of the hardest decisions you'll ever face in life is choosing whether to walk away or try harder.
Unknown

Roadside Pursuit:

Look at your calendar. When will you plan time for your soul to stop, listen, ask and stroll through this special time of year? Schedule time for you and God to be together at least for 15 minutes during the next week.

Roadside Rest Stop:

Lord of peace, rest, and joy: Help me see your way in my path in your light and experience your direction with my every step.

Finding Wisdom at our Crossroads

Listen as Wisdom calls out! Hear as understanding raises her voice! On the hilltop along the road, she takes her stand at the crossroads.
Proverbs 8: 1-2 NLT

One of the gifts we discover as we face crossroads in life is wisdom. As these verses show us, Wisdom takes her stand at crossroads. This is where we will find her.

What wisdom will we hear during the Advent holidays?

In the days before Christmas, many churches sing and pray what is called the O Antiphons. This ancient form of entering the holidays season can be sung with others or on your own. The words and chanting turn our focus away from our indecisions and anxieties and toward the magnificent, loving God.

This Christmas tradition arises from the prophecies found in the book of Isaiah, showing us various names for the coming Messiah.

The first O Antiphon sung each year is called O Sapientia or O Wisdom, referring to Isaiah 11: 2: "The Spirit of the Lord shall rest on him, the Spirit of Wisdom and understanding, the spirit of counsel and might, the spirit of the knowledge of the fear of the Lord. His delight shall be in the fear of the Lord."

The words sung are these;

O Wisdom of our God Most High,
guiding creation with power and love:
come to teach us the path of knowledge!

Finding wisdom involves listening deeply. We turn off the world's chatter and hush our internal whining and ranting fears.

Deep listening to God and to our hearts takes time to cultivate. We have to become still enough for self-reflection and prayer. Recognizing and spending time with our various, and at times conflicting emotions bring peace and clearer decision-making. When we pause, we hear God clearer and uncover his spirit of wisdom.

Let wisdom be your guide this season – and every time you approach crossroads. God's word will guide us with power and love and teach us along our paths.

Roadside Billboard:

Wisdom is the reward you get for a lifetime of listening when you'd have preferred to talk.
Doug Larson

Roadside Pursuit:

Review the past few months and write down what you have learned. Recording the bits and pieces of wisdom we find along the way will add up to deep knowledge that helps us in discerning our next right step or direction to take. Where are you finding wisdom in your life? Listen and pay attention.

Roadside Rest Stop:

God of Wisdom, you never fail to provide light for my journey. Help me hear you in the moments of my life and especially during the busy holidays. Open my heart to experience your presence and thank you for teaching me your ways.

Road Construction Ahead

Pass through, pass through the gates! Prepare the way for the people.
Build up, build up the highway! Remove the stones.
Raise a banner for the nations.
Isaiah 62:10

The joke goes like this: In my home state of Ohio, there are four seasons – Fall, Winter, Spring, and Orange Barrel.

When construction takes over our roads in the summer, the orange barrels multiply. In some areas, there are more orange barrels than people. These colorful nuisances decorate our roads like wild flowers scattered along the highway.

It's all necessary preparation and prevention, helping the road serve its purpose.

In our journeys, we encounter times of orange barrels. They slow us down, make us take detours, block the crossroads where we thought we would be turning. Life's orange barrels are unexpected illnesses or injuries, necessary obligations, and commitments. They all take us off the journey we thought we would be on.

Holidays are supposed to be a time of peace and joy, yet this time of year also presents obstacles. The rushing of this season heightens our anxiety and disrupts our routines. Changes in family calendars, illnesses, and overloaded schedules interfere with expected plans and comforting customs.

As I write these devotions, we have plans to see my son, daughter-in-law and my precious grandson to celebrate Christmas – five months after the fact. Every time this past winter we planned our Christmas get-together, a major snow storm arrived. Christmas in spring? Yes, that is an orange barrel for me right now.

We have our life planned and hold certain expectations, then something happens to force us to slow down, stop, and even change our intended path. We have to make decisions when not all the facts are known, and the answers are unclear.

Our Bible verse today shows Isaiah recognized there would be times to build up the highway and remove the stones. He reminds us that obstacles will block our way. He encourages us to expect these times, to pass on by, and not to forget to raise the banner of praise.

We survive life's orange barrels in the same way: read the signs, knowing changes are approaching. On the road we see the warnings – slow traffic ahead or right lane closed. Our senses heighten as we pay attention to our surroundings and those traveling the same way as us. We follow the direction of the flagger pointing the way as we prepare to enter times of obstacles and rebuilding.

As we come into busy seasons and encounter unexpected obstacles, we remember to slow down and change lanes if needed. We consider if we can remove the stones that block our way. Slowly, we keep our eyes and hearts on our purpose in life: knowing God and making him known to others.

We lift the banner of praise for the God who is with us in all seasons, especially those littered with orange barrels.

Roadside Billboard:

Every human being is under construction from conception to death. Billy Graham

Roadside Pursuit:

List the orange barrels you are seeing in your life now. What are the road signs telling you to do? Pay attention to the nudges and whispers from God.

Roadside Rest Stop:

Lord, we get frustrated when we have to slow down in our lives, or when unexpected events abruptly force us to change. Help us to hear you, follow you and pay attention to your guidance in times of change, detours, and experiences in this busy holiday season. We praise your name.

Blind Begging at the Crossroads

As Jesus approached Jericho, a blind man was sitting by the roadside begging. When he heard the crowd going by, he asked what was happening. They told him, "Jesus of Nazareth is passing by."

He called out, "Jesus, Son of David, have mercy on me!"

Those who led the way rebuked him and told him to be quiet, but he shouted all the more, "Son of David, have mercy on me!"

Jesus stopped and ordered the man to be brought to him. When he came near, Jesus asked him, "What do you want me to do for you?"

"Lord, I want to see," he replied.

Jesus said to him, "Receive your sight; your faith has healed you." Immediately he received his sight and followed Jesus, praising God.
Luke 18: 35-43

The blind beggar sat at the edge of the road, on the margins of life. Others told him stories about Jesus, and now this miracle-maker passed by. He shouted to Jesus in a desperate prayer. "Jesus, Son of David, have mercy on me."

Jesus stopped and listened. Then Jesus asked. "What do you want me to do for you?"

Jesus asks us the same question. What do you want me to do for you? This powerful question to ponder and to pray about adds clarity in times of discernment. Jesus asks us directly and is open to a specific request. What do we want?

We often are overwhelmed by life's confusing chaos and, like the blind man, lose our vision. We lose sight of what the holidays deeply mean and focus more on holiday decorations, the right gifts, the perfect food to take to the neighbors, and the expectations of family members. Busyness brings blindness.

We call out with the only words we can muster up from the darkness in our blurry vision of reality. Lord have mercy on me!

Jesus will stop and listen to our cries. He understands. He asks each of us, "What do you want me to do for you?"

Tell God your specific desire at this crossroad. If you can't name it, ask him to help you find the words. Trust him with that wound festering in your heart for too long. Invite him to come and spend time with you during the holiday and help you find the peace and joy he wants each of us to know.

During the holidays, old hurts, new offenses, and demanding expectations obscure our sight. Call to Jesus. He will answer and may surprise you with his question: What do you want me to do? Tell him.

Roadside Billboard:

Ask and it will be given to you; seek and you will find; knock and the door will be opened to you. For everyone who asks receives; the one who seeks finds; and to the one who knocks, the door will be opened.
Matthew 7:7

Roadside Pursuit:

Ask God for something specific during this holiday season. Write out your answer to Jesus' question: What do you want me to do for you?

Roadside Rest Stop:

Open the ears of my heart to hear you this Christmas, Lord. Give me sight, help me see you in all the celebrations, in the people I encounter, and in the peaceful moments at home and church. I ask you today for _____ and am grateful for your invitation to approach you with my request.

Unintentional Outcomes from Obstructed Intentions

As they were walking along the road, a man said to him, "I will follow you wherever you go."
Luke 9: 57

"The road to hell is paved with good intentions" is a proverb many of us know all too well. We genuinely want to follow Jesus. We want to be obedient. We know God's way is the only way.

Why do we fail? The gap between deciding and doing looms large for humans. We can't do it on our strength. Our limited wisdom fails us. And, to be honest, we neglect to take the right steps out of convenience, weakness, or laziness.

Not fulfilling our intention isn't always our fault either. As we travel along our life paths, we carry our hopes and dreams along with us. Sometimes, our journey takes unexpected turns due to outside forces, unexpected illnesses/injuries, or circumstances out of our control. Whether from our faults or external circumstances, a worthwhile plan abruptly stops.

Like the man in this verse, we walk along the road intent on following Christ wherever he goes, then distractions, human desires, and laziness direct our actions. Maybe this disciple became ill or God called him to serve elsewhere. We don't know.

All we know is good intentions don't always materialize. When we enter the intersection of unexpected changes, we experience failure, disappointment, and possibly shame.

Instead of focusing on the unexpected, what if we asked God to use this moment to teach us? What gifts emerge from our unplanned detour? Ask the Lord what your next step should be. Keep going? Let go? Go in a new direction?

The Christmas story overflows with examples of unintentional outcomes. Mary never expected her pregnancy. Joseph intended to divorce her quietly. The shepherds expected a routine, boring night. The Wise Men thought they would return on the same route they first traveled.

No one anticipated God would send his son as a baby.

Consider what Christmas plans are part of your upcoming intentions. Do you have people you want to visit? Cards to write? Just the perfect dinner to plan and cook? Decorating to the hilt when less may be more beautiful?

Along the road to Christmas, what are our intentions? In our journeys through the holidays, or any place along the way, our wonderfully designed intentions may hit an obstruction. Our Christmas gift from God may be this change in plans, holding a lesson for our growth. We decide how to make the most of roadblocks along the way.

Stay open to God's possibilities. Listen for the Lord. Find the holy in the hindrances.

Roadside Billboard:

Each day holds a surprise. But only if we expect it can we see, hear, or feel it when it comes to us.
Let's not be afraid to receive each day's surprise, whether it comes to us as sorrow or as joy.
It will open a new place in our hearts, a place where we can welcome friends and celebrate more fully our shared humanity.
Henri J.M. Nouwen

Roadside Pursuit:

Make a list of what you intend to accomplish this holiday season. What is realistic? What is past its time and needs to be set aside? Talk with family members about what they want. Name the few items that warm your heart at Christmas. What will draw you closer to God during the busy holidays?

Roadside Rest Stop:

Lord, remind me what is important. Help me keep my eyes and heart only on you. Guide me in completing what you call me to do during this season, and in all moments. And grant me the wisdom to listen to you and learn what you are teaching me.

The Intersection of Kindness and Love

A priest happened to be going down the same road, and when he saw the man, he passed by on the other side.
Luke 10: 31

Doing the right thing sounds perfect, a goal to strive for. But doing the right thing often involves inconvenience, takes our time and perhaps our money, and interrupts our plans.

The story of the Good Samaritan (Luke 10: 25-37) takes place along a road traveled by many sojourners. A priest passes by an injured man lying in the road and decides to cross over to the other side of the road, ignoring him. He chose not to be involved or to help or serve.

A second traveler glanced over at the man, helpless along the sideline, and chose to continue on his own path.

How am I like these wanderers? Do you ever see yourself as the priest? The other traveler? At times I find myself deciding not to serve, help, or reach out, using many excuses – not enough time, not enough money, or just plain compassion fatigue. What can one person do?

One person can make a difference in the lives of others, especially those ignored, isolated, and unconnected.

The Samaritan stops, interrupts his journey, and gets involved. He goes beyond what is expected in helping the injured man by taking him for help and even paying for his care. This man came to a crossroad and decided to change direction to help another person. He did the right thing. I wonder where he was going, how late he was, and what he gave up in order to help another.

Doing the right thing is never convenient or expedient. This can be especially true during the busy holidays. As Martin Luther King said, "The time is always right to do what is right."

What is God inviting us to do? Prayerfully listen to him. Notice when he nudges you to continue or perhaps change your plans. Take the time to write Christmas greetings to friends, visit a shut-in, bake a surprise for the neighbors, or attend Advent services.

Doing the right thing may change our direction, at least temporarily, but it will make the whole journey better – not only for us, but for others along the way.

We do the right thing because God asks us to be love – his love for others. We may be the only love someone sees in our small gestures, kind smiles, or hospital visits. God's love is our compass as we do what is right, even when we don't feel like it, or it disrupts our plans. What appears as an inconvenience to me brings hope and life to another.

The challenge is to pay attention and ask what is important. We have to stop in our travels and choose to practice kindness and love vs. doing nothing.

How does the intersection of kindness and love change our intentions? Who needs your compassion, connection, and comfort during the holidays?

Roadside Billboard:

My basic principle is that you don't make decisions because they are easy; you don't make them because they are cheap; you don't make them because they're popular; you make them because they're right. Theodore Hesburgh

Roadside Pursuit:

How will you respond to those in need this Christmas? Take a moment to focus not on all the things you need to get done, but who around you has an unmet need. Stop at the intersection of kindness and love and do the right thing.

Roadside Rest Stop:

Loving Lord, wake me up to knowing when to do the right thing, especially in times I hedge, thinking of the inconvenience, time, and money involved. Help me hear you and discern how you want me to act in all the circumstances of my life.

The Direct Route

Now he had to go through Samaria. So he came to a town in Samaria called Sychar, near the plot of ground Jacob had given to his son Joseph. Jacob's well was there, and Jesus, tired as he was from the journey, sat down by the well. It was about noon.
When a Samaritan woman came to draw water, Jesus said to her, "Will you give me a drink?"
John 4: 5-7

Our GPS arrived loaded with many options. We can set the menu, so the directions will take us on the shortest route, the interstate route, fastest route, or the most scenic route. We can choose to avoid tolls or follow adventurous dirt roads. We can add stops for refreshing breaks or unusual tourist destinations.

Most often my family chooses the direct route. Jesus did so too in today's verses.

The road through Samaria near the town of Sychar is the shortest route from Galilee to Jerusalem. The unusual note about this road Jesus chose was most Jews at that time took the longer, indirect route east of the Jordan River because they disliked the Samaritans. For many centuries, these two groups of people had been enemies, so most Jews went out of their way, deciding to take the lengthier path to avoid a problematic relationship.

John does not explain why Jesus decided to go this way. He simply writes that Jesus "had to go." Jesus may have known he was to meet this woman and transform her life and those around her with his loving presence.

Jesus simply followed God's will and took the direct route, knowing the path would lead to uncomfortable and uneasy interactions. Jesus paid attention to those around him and welcomed whomever he met along his journey.

As we travel in life and through the holidays, let's pay attention too. Maybe God is inviting us into awkward dealings with family and wants us to keep our eyes and our hearts open. The direct route may put us into the path of an annoying neighbor or the one who talks incessantly.

Pay attention to the store clerk and smile. Compliment the next person you meet. Pause and savor the giggle of children and songs of Christmas. Smell the aroma of baking sugar cookies and feel the touch of an elder's hands.

Holidays take us into direct contact with people and situations we like to avoid. This season also brings us the gift of opportunity for love, patience, and less ego. Like Jesus, tired from his journey, we too stop to rest and find an opportunity to refresh another soul.

Like the woman at the well, pause and drink Jesus' living water along the direct route. Following God's direct path may bring us into direct contact with the one who needs us the most.

Roadside Billboard:

It's not only moving that creates new starting points. Sometimes all it takes is a subtle shift in perspective, an opening of the mind, an intentional pause and reset, or a new route to start to see new options and new possibilities.
Kristin Armstrong

Roadside Pursuit:

Pay attention to those who cross your path today. Write in your journal: What did you see, hear, touch, or taste today that made you stop, look and listen? Describe your path in life – right now, is it a direct route or out of your way?

Roadside Rest Stop:

God, we need your guidance. Be our GPS. Wake us up to notice those you give us along this direct route through the holidays. May we be your hands and love to others along our way.

Crossroad Decisions and Turning Points

Take Note of the Signposts

Set up road signs; put up guideposts.
Take note of the highway, the road that you take.
Jeremiah 31: 21

I don't remember driving home. I left work that day with my mind crammed with to-dos that I didn't get done and a crazy schedule facing me at home. I thought about the piles of laundry, dinner to prepare, and the kids' conflicting schedules. My head, hands, and heart morphed into a three-ring circus as I juggled work, family, and home.

And the holidays fast approached too.

I pulled into the driveway and realized I didn't remember one single thing about the drive home. How did I get here? Did I even stop at that intersection? I drove mentally on autopilot, so focused on what had happened and what was about to occur, I missed the present.

This phenomenon accelerates during the Christmas rush. Commitments cram our calendars and craniums. Expectations explode our minds and hearts. We yearn for the gift of peace from Bethlehem, but only find an empty promise of "maybe later."

Crossroads often display stop signs. We may also encounter signs telling us to yield. Flashing lights warning us to slow down.

We can take these signposts in our spiritual journey as an invitation to pause and savor the present. We hold the moment we are in right now in our open hands. We breathe in the now and breathe out the next.

Staying in the present involves watching our speed and direction. Be mindful in the moment. Challenge yourself to try at least three times a day to stop and notice your internal and external surroundings.

Take a moment just to sit by the fire. Gaze at the decorated tree. Ponder the nativity set. Sit in the church sanctuary when no one is around. Breathe.

Look around you as you drive. See the snow on the pine trees. Laugh at a neighbor's decorated yard. Smile and wave at neighbors. Savor as much as you can. Where are you seeing God today?

Life unfolds in the present. Too often we miss it and squander the sacred seconds of our lives.

Take note on the journey we are on. Watch the signposts. Stop. Yield. Slow down.

We only have the present.

Roadside Billboard

Pay attention to the beauty surrounding you.
Anne Lamott

Roadside Pursuit

Breathe. Stop several times today to savor the moment. What do you see right before you? Let your senses ground you in the present. Where are you experiencing God in Advent and Christmas?

Roadside Rest Stop

Wake me up, Lord. Help me be mindful of you in the present. Thank you for the gift of breathing. Resting. Beholding the moment. Moments with you.

What are the Crossroads?

***I've brought you today to the crossroads of Blessing and Curse.
Deuteronomy 11: 26 (The Message)***

Ever see those bright, hand-painted signs pointing north, south, east and west, listing all the miles to exotic places? The green sign with the iguana tells us the beach is one mile in this direction. The red one points to Paris. We learn Aruba is 1,758 miles to the south.

When we aren't sure where we are heading, our eyes hunt for crossroad signs. We look for where to turn and if we are on the correct route. We discover our present location is at the corner of Main and High Streets or, as this bible verse notes, the point of Blessing and Curse.

I wonder if Mary, when she learned she would give birth to God's son, wondered about the name of her present intersection. Fear and Belief? Obedience and Willfulness? Trust and Doubt?

When we are lost, sometimes names mean nothing to us and may lead to more confusion. But usually knowing our location, naming where we are, helps us get our bearings or brings us to someone who will direct us on our way.

Times of busyness and moments of discernment often bring feelings of being lost and unsure of where we are heading. Our intersection signs might be Should and Must or This Way or That Way.

Though this may seem silly at first, naming our present location with the image of crossroad signs begins to ground us and helps us see our way. I envision myself at a crossroad, knowing the time is right to take a deep breath and pause.

When I am confused and not sure which way to turn, I pause, listen, and look. I rest in God asking for his guidance at least in the next step I should take. I tell him the names of my intersection and how I am feeling.

I want to see the final destination, know where I am heading and receive assurance that I see the end point. But life doesn't work that way most of the time.

I listen. What is God telling me through prayer and scripture? I read and hear the words of wisdom from others in books, sermons, and conversations. I listen to myself too. What is my heart telling me? How should I be true to my desires? Or is this my ego and self-doubt taking control?

Then I look. I look at the crossroads. What is on those signs at this intersection? Hope and Promise? Adventure vs. Comfort? Change and Challenge? I name the choices, the next right steps, and listen once again.

Where are you right now in your life journey? During this holy season, what crossroad are you seeing and seeking?

Roadside Billboard

The cross of Jesus Christ represents the intersection of God's love and God's holiness.
Robert Jeffress

Roadside Pursuit

Name your crossroads. Find two words that describe where you are in life presently. What does that tell you? How would you change them? What is God inviting you to choose for your intersection?

Roadside Rest Stop

Almighty Lord, I am so grateful you are with me no matter where I journey or what direction I wander. Help me see clearly the crossroads I am passing and hear your voice in how to proceed on my path.

Turning Points in Discernment

Then Joseph could no longer control himself before all his attendants, and he cried out, "Have everyone leave my presence!" So there was no one with Joseph when he made himself known to his brothers. And he wept so loudly that the Egyptians heard him, and Pharaoh's household heard about it.

Joseph said to his brothers, "I am Joseph! Is my father still living?" But his brothers were not able to answer him, because they were terrified at his presence.

Then Joseph said to his brothers, "Come close to me." When they had done so, he said, "I am your brother Joseph, the one you sold into Egypt! And now, do not be distressed and do not be angry with yourselves for selling me here, because it was to save lives that God sent me ahead of you. For two years now there has been famine in the land, and for the next five years there will be no plowing and reaping. But God sent me ahead of you to preserve for you a remnant on earth and to save your lives by a great deliverance. Genesis 45: 1-7

Life doesn't always give us the choice of which way to turn. Circumstances are thrust upon us unexpectedly and uninvited.

Joseph didn't choose to travel to Egypt. His brothers sold him into slavery. Joseph didn't choose to become the king's trusted aide. As a slave, he didn't have that freedom, but he made the most of his situation. Joseph could have decided to take revenge on his brothers who betrayed him, but instead, he decided on love and forgiveness. At key turning points, Joseph chose the better way.

When the angel came to Mary, she too chose the better way.

When Joseph, her betrothed, could have rejected her due to her pregnancy, he chose to be at her side.
After worshiping the newborn Christ, the wise men listened to God and chose a different route.

We too find ourselves on unanticipated journeys. We lose our jobs. Illness or injury arrive unexpectedly. Disappointment and disagreement among loved ones threaten to ruin the season of peace.

When circumstances seize our souls, we feel helpless. Fear takes over and dominates our decisions. We feel weak, vulnerable, and powerless. We do have control on one aspect of the situation – the attitude of our mind and heart.

At these types of crossroads, we set our mind on things of God. We make the decision to focus on "whatever is true, whatever is noble, whatever is right, whatever is pure, whatever is lovely, whatever is admirable – if anything is excellent or praiseworthy – think about such things," as Philippians 4: 8 teaches us.

We align our heart with love. God's love when we can't find our own. We chose mercy, forgiveness, and love. We give the other person and ourselves grace, space for God to work in their lives too without our anger.

At turning points, we can choose the better way. Choose a different route. We have the power to decide our mindset about our circumstance. We control the direction of our thoughts and can reframe a situation in order to live the life Christ has offered us.

Turning points create choices. We can't choose our circumstances, but we can choose our conduct.

Roadside Billboard

May your choices reflect your hopes, not your fears.
Nelson Mandela

Roadside Pursuit

Take time during this season to assess your attitude when situations don't go your way. Is it time to let go of past grudges and hurts and move on to healing? Where can you choose mercy, love, and forgiveness?

Roadside Rest Stop

Lord, as I encounter turning points in my life, help me be aware when my mind misleads me. Shower me with your wisdom and strength to let go of emotions that arise from powerlessness, and with your help purify my mindset to find you in every circumstance.

Crossroad Detours

When Pharaoh let the people go, God did not lead them on the road through the Philistine country, though that was shorter. For God said, "If they face war, they might change their minds and return to Egypt." So God led the people around by the desert road toward the Red Sea. The Israelites went up out of Egypt ready for battle.
Exodus 13: 17-18

The highway sign warned us that the left lane was closed four miles ahead. My hubby dutifully merged into the right, and I began to brace myself for the number one pet peeve in his life. He gets angry at the drivers who wait until the last minute to change lanes, then expects everyone who obeyed earlier to let them into line.

Sometimes we get warning that a lane change or detour is ahead, and if we pay attention, we prepare and adjust. I have traveled on roads where we have only been given a short distance to merge and am surprised to shift quickly.

Detours are opportunities to see things in new light.

How do we react to the detours we encounter in life, such as unexpected news, change in major plans, or illness or injury? How do we face the detours that arrive during the Christmas rush? We create elaborate plans for the perfect holiday, only to be sidetracked by the unforeseen.

As Mary and Joseph traveled to Bethlehem, I wonder if they knew it would be the birthplace of their son. No room in the inn. Who helped them with this new experience of labor and delivery?

If it were me, after the birth, I would want to return to Nazareth and get settled. I would need family around for support and to share in the joy of a new baby. I would yearn for the normalcy and comfort of home.

But once again, a detour appeared for Mary and Joseph. In a dream, God warned them not to go home but to head to the safety of Egypt. In today's verse, God directed the Israelites on a different route to their new land. And, on the night of Jesus' birth, the shepherds certainly had a detour thrust upon them.

Detours happen. Most of the time, we can't barge through the "road closed" sign but have to take the route given us. Taking the detour is the only way to keep moving forward.

We take that step ahead into new territory and God goes with us. We may even find surprising gifts along the way if we stay open to see what God has in store for us. A change of direction may lead to an upgrade of destination.

Roadside Billboard

A truly happy person is one who can enjoy the scenery on a detour. Anonymous

Roadside Pursuit

What detours are you facing right now? How do the holidays create more changes or increased anxiety about the unexpected? What can you do to manage your heart and mind?

Roadside Rest Stop

Lord of peace and wisdom, open my eyes to see the gifts found in the detours in my journey. Show me how to make the best out of the messes along the way. And help me to keep my heart focused on you and where you are leading me.

Unexpected Turns

About noon, King Agrippa, as I was on the road, I saw a light from heaven, brighter than the sun, blazing around me and my companions.
Acts 26: 13

Paul's life unexpectedly turned on the road to Damascus. He had his life planned. To be powerful, influential and make a contribution to what he valued and believed. God changed Paul and put him on a new path.

I wonder what Mary and Joseph talked about on the road to Bethlehem. Their lives were disrupted by pregnancy and now the requirement to report for the census. This path was not what they planned earlier in their relationship. The unexpected pivot altered their journey forever.

Nothing would be the same for any of these people.

Unexpected turns occur any time of the year. But during the stress of Christmas, a death, illness, injury, extra company, extra work, changes in routines ... even burning the neighbors' Christmas gifts in the oven, or dropping the bowl of salad all over the floor as everyone sits down for Christmas Eve dinner ... these disruptions are especially jarring to the peace we are supposed to enjoy during this season.

It's not just your own expectations, but others' expectations that can throw you off course. Unfortunately, you can't be two places at once. And you can't meet everyone's demands.

"If you want to make God laugh, tell him your plans" is a funny saying seen on social media.

A sharp left turn on our journey. An unforeseen change. An unexpected and unrequested redirection. When our life spins out of control, what is God inviting us to learn?

Unexpected turns remind us who is in control. God is. I continually have to remember that as I struggle to think that I am in charge. I rest with my hands open, holding all my circumstances and the people around me. I imagine giving them to God. I hold them out lightly, allowing God to grace me with peace and perseverance for the season.

We can pause and tell ourselves what is happening, and acknowledge the emerging and demanding emotions within our hearts. This action makes it easier to let go of the situation.

My unexpected turn twirls into thanksgiving. I am grateful that the One who knows best is the One who is in charge. Paul learned that fact. Mary and Joseph witnessed this reality in their lives. And no matter the time of year, we too can trust in the process and that our journey is in God's hands. He has many surprises for those who follow him and are open to his gifts in unexpected turns.

Roadside Billboard

In moments of surprise, we catch at least a glimpse of the joy to which gratefulness opens the door.
David Steindl-Rast

Roadside Pursuit

What unexpected turns are your experiencing? What could be their gifts? Where is God surprising you right now?

Roadside Rest Stop

Caring God, help me remember you are in charge, and I am forever in your loving hands. Thank you for the surprises you have given me along the way, and help me see you in all my circumstances

Crossroad Courage and Cautions

And who knows but that you have come to your royal position for such a time as this? Esther 4: 14b

Travel light. Only carry what you need. Extra baggage weighs you down.

Good advice for any type of journey and especially valued wisdom for our travels in life.

Two necessary items to pack in our life's backpack are courage and caution. These traits help us along the way and at each intersection of discernment.

Courage means to take the time and risk to explore the question around a decision. We pause and listen to God and our hearts.

Caution gives us insight in weighing the pros and cons to discern to our next steps. We seek out wisdom from wise counsel, again listening with both our hearts and our minds wide open.

Our Bible verse today tells the story found in the Old Testament about Esther, a queen in Persia. The king doesn't know she is Jewish. Her uncle Mordecai refuses to bow down and worship the king, provoking the king's assistant, Haram, to make a policy to kill her uncle and all the Jewish people.

Queen Esther knew she could stop this and make a difference, but her decision took courage and caution. After praying and fasting, she took the risk of going to the king and telling him, thus saving her uncle and the Jewish people.

Courage and Caution marked the crossroads of discernment.

The Christmas story abounds with people entering this same intersection. Mary says yes. Joseph obeys. They listen to God and flee to Egypt. The shepherds rush to see the newborn king. The Wise men follow the star.

God gives us the courage and caution we need when facing decisions. Unwrap these gifts, not only at a Christmas, but all year long. Tuck them into your backpack even as you travel light.

Courage and Caution marked the crossroads of discernment. Courage and caution – two essentials for life's travel.

Roadside Billboard

Acts of bravery don't always take place on battlefields. They can take place in your heart, when you have the courage to honor your character, your intellect, your inclinations, and yes, your soul by listening to its clean, clear voice of direction instead of following the muddied messages of a timid world.
Anna Quindlen

Roadside Pursuit

Write out your deepest desire and how you feel God wants you to live your life. What decisions are your facing currently? How would courage and caution help you along your journey?

Roadside Rest Stop

God of Courage, God of Caution, thank you for these gifts you've given me. I taste their goodness and open my hand for more from your endless supply. Help me use them in discerning my next right direction in life.

Touching Calm in the Chaos

They beached the boat at Gennesaret and tied up at the landing. As soon as they got out of the boat, word got around fast. People ran this way and that, bringing their sick on stretchers to where they heard he was. Wherever he went, village or town or country crossroads, they brought their sick to the marketplace and begged him to let them touch the edge of his coat – that's all. And whoever touched him became well.
Mark 6: 53-56 The Message

I don't like to shop in the stores in December. Finding a place to park is difficult. People live on the edge of fatigue and anger. Madness rules at the check-out counters. And we have all seen on the news, and perhaps in person, people yanking and fighting over the last toy available.

When our environment swirls with chaos, we lose any sense of order and direction. No wonder we feel lost and confused on our paths!

Chaos reigned at Gennesaret too. People heard the healer, the Messiah, Jesus of Nazareth arrived. They heard stories and rumors of others being healed. They rushed to bring their ill loved ones to be close to him.

The crowds followed Jesus wherever he went. They listened to his stories. They sought him when they didn't know where to find him.

All the people wanted was to touch Jesus. They knew this personal contact with him would transform their lives. Just a simple encounter would change everything. Meeting Jesus has that effect in ancient times and today too.

Touching Jesus during crazy chaos calms our souls. The crucial and core tool of compassion is expressed in touch.

During Christmas rush, and throughout our lives, we can follow Jesus. We can listen to his stories. We can seek him even when we can't find him. We can keep our eyes and hearts on him, not the frenzy churning around and inside us.

Jesus will find us. We don't have to journey far. He will take our hands. He will heal our hearts and make us well. Jesus' presence is the touch of God upon us.

What a gift God gives us. God sent his Son to bring peace and healing to the broken and chaotic world. All we have to do is follow Jesus and reach out to touch him.

Touching Jesus transforms chaos into calm.

Roadside Billboard

Too often we underestimate the power of a touch, a smile, a kind word, a listening ear, an honest compliment, or the smallest act of caring, all of which have the potential to turn a life around.
Leo Buscaglia

Roadside Pursuit

God is closer than the vein in your neck. ... Begin by placing your first and second fingers on your throat's jugular vein. ... What better way to be mindful of the nearness of the Presence than to actually feel it vibrating on your fingertips? To gain the attention of God, your intimate Beloved, does not require bellowing prayers, clanging bells, or thunderous pipe-organ preludes. A silent sensual touch can profoundly awaken you to God's perpetual attention to you and your needs.
Edward Hays

Roadside Rest Stop

Compassionate Lord, touch my heart today. Slow me enough to experience your presence and lay your hands upon my skittish soul. Thank you for calming the chaos surrounding this season and throughout my journey. You are the connection I need to find peace.

Lessons from the Intersections

With her two daughters-in-law, she (Naomi) left the place where they had been living and set out on the road that would take them back to the land of Judah. Ruth 1: 7

Going home. This time of year often involves trips to visit families near and far. Sometimes the trip overflows with joy, laughter, and love. Other times bittersweet sadness descends upon our souls, weary from travel, stress, and unmet needs.

Where do you find home?

Naomi returned home after losing her sons and husband. She traveled with her two daughters-in-law for part of the journey. Ruth stayed with her until they reach the place Naomi immigrated from originally. This homeland provided a sense of return for Naomi, but was new and unfamiliar to Ruth.

Where did Ruth find home in this new place with different rituals, unknown customs, and strange faces? The answer involves finding connection and a sense of community in a place.

Where do you find home? Is it the location of your birth? Where you now pay taxes? Where family is found? Where do you connect with community?

Pico Iyer said, "Where is your home? I literally couldn't point to any physical construction. My home would have to be whatever I carried around inside me ... home, we know, is not just the place where you happen to be born. It's the place where you become yourself."

Where do you find home this Christmas? Think beyond the physical location. Is home where you experience God in a deeper way? A place where you feel accepted, safe, and loved?

The arms of God protect us and welcome us near, even in unknown and new places. His love grounds us in our center and gives us roots that will stay with us no matter how far we travel.

Connect with God and you will find home.

Roadside Billboard

Unraveling external selves and coming home to our real identity is the true meaning of soul work.
Sue Monk Kidd

Roadside Pursuit

Write out your definition of home. Where and when do you experience connection and community? Take that experience with you as your travel home this season.

Roadside Rest Stop

Loving Lord, I come home to you. In your arms, I connect with you and find the completion of what I miss in the world. You are home to my weary heart. You are where I find rest, refreshment, and joy.

Daily Guidebook

Now the Berean Jews were of more noble character than those in Thessalonica, for they received the message with great eagerness and examined the scriptures every day to see if what Paul said was true.
Acts 17: 11

"Examined the scriptures every day." What dedication to knowing what is true and what is not! The scriptures are our guidebook on the road of discernment and decisions at the crossroads.

The Jewish followers of Jesus who lived in Berea listened to Paul and Silas, taking in the good news while studying the scriptures. The missionaries traveled to this small city located about 50 miles from Thessalonica on the eastern side of Mount Olympus.

The Bereans enthusiastically examined the scriptures to learn God's words for their lives.

The wise men traveled from the East, seeking the Messiah they heard had been born in Bethlehem. They studied the stars to know the direction of their path. We too have a guide for our path – the Bible.

Studying the word of God provides the light in dark times and direction when we feel lost. The word of God directs our path and helps us in our discernment.

Here is some Biblical wisdom for decision-making:

First Thessalonians 5:21-22 tell us to "examine everything carefully; hold fast to that which is good; abstain from every form of evil."

John advises us in these words: "Do not believe every spirit but test the spirits to see whether they are from God; because many false prophets have gone out into the world." (1 John 4:1)

The Psalmist encourages us, singing these words from Psalm 119:66: "Teach me good discernment and knowledge, for I believe in Your commandments." What a prayer to remember.

Paul wrote to the Philippians in chapter 3, verses 9-10 with this prayer and wisdom: "And this I pray, that your love may abound still more and more in real knowledge and all discernment, so that you may approve the things that are excellent, in order to be sincere and blameless until the day of Christ."

We are reminded to listen and continually seek in discernment in the book of Proverbs 18: 25: "The heart of the discerning acquires knowledge, for the ears of the wise seek it out."
When facing crossroads of discernment, open the Bible and find a catalog of directions. The Word of God lights your way as your daily guidebook.

Roadside Billboard
God does not exist to answer our prayers, but by our prayers we come to discern the mind of God.
Oswald Chambers

Roadside Pursuit

Find a favorite Bible verse about discernment to use it in the crossroads you encounter. Write it out in your own words. Pray about its guidance. Ask God to use those words to help you decide on your journey.

Roadside Rest Stop

Wise and Wondrous Lord, you provide the guidance and wisdom I need to enter all the intersections of life to discern whether to stop, turn or continue straight. I do want to follow your will – help me discern and hear your voice.

Desert Road Encounters

Philip obeyed God and left … And entered the desert roads. Acts 8: 26,36

What are our desert roads?

Life comes with full and empty times. We find ourselves lonely, unproductive and isolated. We can't sense our next steps, full of hollow hopelessness.

Why would God want part of our journey to be through dry, barren times?

Perhaps the answer to this question lies with whom we will meet during these seasons of life.

Philip met the Ethiopian, an interaction nether of them unexpected. The encounter along the way filled the Ethiopian's need and provided an answer for Phillip's life too. Phillip found affirmation for the direction he was going.

What happened to Phillip next? In Acts 21, we find Phillip living in Caesarea and providing housing for Paul as Paul returns from a mission trip on his way to Jerusalem. Knowing his life purpose, Phillip continued in the Lord's work, following and doing God's will.

Our desert moments open our eyes to whom God has put in our paths. Even in dry times, pay attention to the people who cross your path and listen to their stories. Their needs may nourish our needs – a double desert gift.

Jesus spent time in the wilderness before he started his ministry. He wasn't alone. God was with him.

Joseph and Mary journeyed to Egypt to protect Jesus when Herod killed the newborn boys. Though the Bible isn't clear how long this trip to the desert lasted, historians believe they were there from a few months to no more than two years before returning home.

But Mary and Joseph were not alone. God was with them.

Hearing God can be a challenge even in good times, but in the desert, other voices echo in the barrenness. Desert times are opportunities for prayer, retreats, silence, stillness, and journaling – all key practices in hearing God.

Pay attention in desert times. Be mindful of fellow travelers. Who is God bringing to us and what lessons are there for us to learn?

We are not alone in our desert times. God is with us.

Harvest the holy in the hollow desert times.

Roadside Billboard

Listening to God – which is a key part of practicing His presence – is not a method, but a walk with a person.
Leanne Payne

Roadside Pursuit

Write out a description of a desert time you've had or are currently experiencing. What emotions are you feeling? What lessons are you learning?

Roadside Rest Stop

Lord of rest and restoration, thank you for always being with me. Shaping my spirit, even in dry, barren times. Open my heart to find your lesson in desert times. Help me see who you want me to see – to hear their stories, to meet their needs as I am able. Help me harvest the Holy in the hollowness of life.

Narrow Roads

But small is the gate and narrow the road that leads to life, and only a few find it.
Matthew 7: 14

I was certain the GPS was wrong. Her friendly voice told us how to get to our campsite near Yosemite, but the route took a long roundabout highway.

According to the map I was studying, Route 49 provided a direct and much shorter route. My hubby took my advice and we set out on this new road. I heard stories about how GPS misled travelers and had been double-checking all her directions on this trip. We second-guessed the expert.

Wrong decision! The steep road we chose to travel became very narrow and steep as it curved around the mountain. I prayed the whole way we wouldn't meet another car coming in the other direction as there would be no room for two.

We didn't speak as our minds focused on the road. We concentrated, and we prayed as we slowly eased along our way. And did I say we prayed? I clutched the door tensely and gritted my teeth. No place to turn around. Once we started, we had to keep going. We dragged our camper and I knew the road would be better traversed without heavy baggage.

We made it safely to our campground but were exhausted from the tension of the trip. We failed to follow the better route.

Jesus advises us on our journey to enter the small gate and that our road to life will be narrow. He invites us to reach the destination he has created for us. We must travel a specific road through his gate. We listen to his voice of wisdom as Jesus is the way, the truth, and the life.

Our paths in life narrow even further with the busyness and crazy schedule of Christmas time. To enjoy this journey through the joys of our savior's birth, slow down and listen for his voice. Stay focused. Pray.

I learned quite a lesson that day on that narrow road – go slow, stay focused, travel light, and pray.

Roadside Billboard

Look up, look up, and let your faith continually increase. Let this faith guide you along the narrow path that leads through the gates of the city into the great beyond, the wide, unbounded future of glory that is for the redeemed.
Ellen G. White

Roadside Pursuit

How is this time of year like a narrow road for you? Practice slowing down, staying focused on the reason for the season and traveling light

Roadside Rest Stop

Thank you, Lord, for being with me all the time and especially in the narrow road moments. Steady my walk by reminding me to slow down and stay focused on you. Help me to let go of what I don't need and to travel light, praying all the way.

Strength Along the Way

Nearly all the people in the crowd threw their garments down on the road, giving him a royal welcome. Others cut branches from the trees and threw them down as a welcome mat.
Matthew 21: 8

Palm Sunday commemorated the day Jesus entered Jerusalem riding on the back of a small donkey. The crowds cheered him, treating him as the type of king they expected. They waved palm branches and threw their coats down before him as if he were royalty.

The parade route descended the Mount of Olives, crossing the large cemetery on the left, facing the Holy City. Halfway down the embankment, visitors entered a small chapel where it is said Jesus wept over this sacred crossroad.

The road takes a steep descent into Jerusalem. When we visited the Holy Lands, we walked down the same path. I clung to my hubby's hand, afraid I may slip on the steep, slippery stones. One of our fellow pilgrims couldn't stop her ever-increasing plunge and called for help as she tumbled past us. My hubby extended his hand to grab her, involuntarily yanking all of us forward. We sighed as we regained control over our downward passage, smiling at each other in relief.

As we walked down this road, I kept thinking about how Jesus knew what was coming. He heard the empty cheering while surrounded by death on one side and tears on the other. This path carried Jesus away through people, pomp, and paradox.

In life, we too face crossroads that may lead us down a steep incline. We lose our footing. We tumble out of control. All we can foresee is more plummeting. All we can do is stop and cry.

How did Jesus handle this crossroad in his life? At the bottom of this mountain before the entrance to Jerusalem is the Garden of Gethsemane. Among the olive trees, Jesus prayed: Your will, not mine. He reached out and experienced strength in the presence of God, and in obedience knew he could continue.

Take a moment as we near Christmas to behold the whole story of Jesus' life. His birth, his teachings. His death. His resurrection. Listen to his story, revealing lessons for both the joyous and sorrowful times in our own lives. Turn to prayer and ask for strength during our sinking times.

God will extend his hand to grab us and help us contain the pace of our path. In our tears, we can pray "your will, not mine." And find strength in obedience with God.

Roadside Billboard

Courage doesn't always roar. Sometimes courage is the little voice at the end of the day that says, "I'll try again tomorrow."
Mary Anne Radmacher

Roadside Pursuit

How do you pray in the out-of-control moments of life? Locate a photograph of the Mount of Olive descent and reread this passage from Matthew. How do the words strengthen you for this journey?

Roadside Rest Stop

Lord, reach out your strong arms and slow my hectic pace. Too much around me seems out of control and crazy, ironically in the season of peace and joy. Bring back my heart to hear your voice, experience your presence, and find strength for each step of the way.

Disrupted Destinations

Jesus prayed, "Father, remove this cup from me. But please, not what I want. What do you want?"
Luke 22: 42

The video on the evening news captivated me. A section of a high bridge collapsed, plunging several cars into the deep water and leaving one car dangling by its back tires. The blue Chevy swayed in the wind and teetered toward a fatal tumble into the deep.

The road abruptly ended, leaving those involved with dramatic changes and upheavals. In our lives, we too enter unanticipated crossroads where either direction isn't our wish or desire.

Life isn't always what we want. We hit detours and destruction we didn't expect or ask for. Our paths come to a complete standstill with mudslides, potholes, and damage. We stop in our tracks, weighed down with helplessness and hopelessness.

How do we continue? How do we know the next right step for our journey? How do we recover and move onward?

Jesus knew his direction only led one destination – to his arrest, beatings, and death. But he also knew where to turn for strength. God.

Jesus talked with God about his fate, but then surrendered his next steps to God. "But please, not what I want. What do you want?"

God is the only answer when the foundation beneath our feet gives way and we plunge into darkness. He will be with us. His strength provides for us. He lights our next steps along the way.

Dark and difficult times demand daring and divine trust.

Mary and Joseph trusted their uncertain future to an infallible God. Jesus knew his mission and gave his all for God's will. When the road collapses and we are suddenly disrupted on our journey, God will be there to catch us and set us once again on firm foundations. In these times, we reach out in surrender and prayer.

We relinquish; God restores.

Roadside Billboard

In the middle of difficulty lies opportunity.
Albert Einstein

Roadside Pursuit

Recall how God has helped you through difficult times in the past. Remembering those promised kept will give you strength for the future.

Roadside Rest Stop

Powerful Lord, help me to remember how you never leave me and always provide for me along my journey. When I feel lost and unsettled in changing times, I cling to you, my unchangeable strength.

Christmas Crossroads and Beyond

Servant Discernment

"I am the Lord's servant," Mary answered. "May your word to me be fulfilled." Then the angel left her. Luke 1: 38

The stories of the first Christmas provide us with wisdom for our journeys.

One of the greatest commitments to obeying God is found in the story of the angel visiting Mary, telling her she would bear God's son. Don't you wonder all the different and overwhelming emotions and thoughts Mary experienced during this time?

As an unmarried, expectant woman, she could have been rejected by Joseph, her family, and society. Friends may have shunned her and gossiped about her. She faced ridicule, insults, and even stoning.

Yet she trusted and obeyed.

The crossroads Mary entered arrived abruptly and unexpectantly. Mary listened, asked, and obeyed. Mary demonstrates a servant heart.

A servant heart asks, "What do you want, Lord? You, not me." Then a person with such a spirit trusts and obeys, following God in each step.

Mary listened to God's words from the angel. She wondered. She knew she was "greatly troubled." She asked questions. "How can this be?" She listened deeply, and then trusted and obeyed.

We can model Mary when we find ourselves in the midst of sudden, bewildering circumstances. When we can't even begin to decipher which way to turn. When without warning, we arrive at a fork in our path and face uncertainty about our next steps.

Like Mary, we wonder. Be honest with God and name the emotions erupting in our hearts.

Like Mary, we ask questions. We seek God's wisdom.

Like Mary, we listen. We search God's word for guidance. We enter prayer grateful for whatever answers emerge.

Like Mary, we trust and obey.

God rarely reveals his entire plan, but he will shine the light on our next step. God directs our path and stays with us. God's job is to create the way. Our job is to trust and obey.

Roadside Billboard

Faith is taking the first step even when you don't see the whole staircase.
Martin Luther King

Roadside Pursuit

Reread the entire story of the angel's visit to Mary. What word resonated with your spirit? How is God inviting you to grow in trust and obedience?

Roadside Rest Stop

Lord, forgive me when I fail to trust and obey you. Thank you for listening when I wonder and ask questions. Help me to hear you and give me wisdom and strength to obey.

Foggy Discernment

But after he had considered this, an angel of the Lord appeared to him in a dream and said, "Joseph son of David, do not be afraid to take Mary home as your wife, because what is conceived in her is from the Holy Spirit.
Matthew 1: 20

Northwest Ohio is known for its thick fog. Schools lose more days to the soupy atmosphere than snow covered winter highways some years. The fog arrives quickly and may stay for days.

No one is surprised at one or two-hour school delays on a foggy morning. Many times, as the morning creeps along and the fog still lingers, the haze cancels the school day. We laugh, because in our imagination the fog knows school has been canceled, so it will soon disappear and a sunny day commences. I think the fog and the students collaborate on this scheme.

The reason schools are delayed or canceled is low visibility. The highways aren't safe. Drivers miss stop signs. A clear vision ahead isn't possible from the driver's seat. Even the sounds of approaching traffic bend and warp our sense of distance.

Joseph must have felt that way when he learned his fiancée, Mary, was pregnant. Then he learned she conceived this child through the Holy Spirit. He had to wonder about their safety. Why him? Why her? A confusing, murky time descended upon his life's path and his well-intended plans.

We too have foggy times in our travels. A period of uncertainty. Confusion. The only sight we see ahead is messy and hazy. We aren't sure of our next step.

When we drive in fog and come to an intersection, the best practice is to stop, listen, and proceed slowly. We pay extra careful attention to noises piecing into the fog, looking for any hints of something coming. We go slowly forward, testing each move.

Discernment in unclear, foggy times requires the same steps. Stop and pause in stillness. Listen deeply. Then go slowly forward, aware of God's gentle touch as he guides us through cloudy confusion. God will be with us, showing us the way.

When fog fills our view, God guides us through.

Roadside Billboard

Faith is like radar that sees through the fog – the reality of things at a distance that the human eye cannot see.
Corrie ten Boom

Roadside Pursuit

How will you use the practices of stillness, listening, and slowness in times when you can't see your next step?

Roadside Rest Stop

God of light and clarity, I trust you to show me the way. Give me the patience to pause and be still with you, listening to your direction. I ask for clearness, safety and guidance along my path.

Waiting with Others at our Crossroads

In a loud voice she exclaimed: "Blessed are you among women and blessed is the child you will bear! But why am I so favored, that the mother of my Lord should come to me? As soon as the sound of your greeting reached my ears, the baby in my womb leaped for joy. Blessed is she who has believed that the Lord would fulfill his promises to her!"
Luke 1: 42-45

Not all crossroads come with burdens and indecision. Sometimes the changes in life bring celebration. Joy multiplies when shared with others. We pause and savor together in the glow of gifts discovered at crossroads.

We join with another person in a transformational experience of the now. We wait and grasp together the meaning of the present time and the present received. Our hearts connect, and joy erupts at the discovery. We bless one another.

Mary and Elizabeth experienced this type of moment together. Mary journeyed to be with her cousin, who was also with child.

The Book of Luke tells us Elizabeth was an older woman married to Zechariah, a member of the Jerusalem priesthood. She was past menopause, her husband was elderly, and she had given up hoping for a child. But Elizabeth's life entered a crossroad with an unexpected turn. She became pregnant to the amazement of all.

Elizabeth's pregnancy brought her solitude, loneliness, and time with her thoughts. When Mary arrived expectant and unexpectedly, I would think Elizabeth would have spilled out her own needs, seeking comfort.

But I never noticed before that the first words out of Elizabeth's mouth when Mary walked into her home were words of blessing:

"You are the most blessed of women, and your child will be blessed."

If this were me, I would have blurted out something about what I needed. I would have bombarded Mary with questions out of my anxiety. This surprising reunion brought forth all sorts of emotions – joy, fear, wonder – but Elizabeth demonstrates the power of offering a blessing in a time of waiting.

We too can be ready to give a blessing when being with others. We discover these blessings after spending time with the God of all blessings. Prayer and time in scripture equip us with an abundant supply of blessings to give away to others. People are so hungry for someone to bless them. We can be that person.

Crossroads contains blessings. These intersections give us a time of becoming and savoring. It is not a time of doing nothing. God shapes us, prepares us, teaches us for what is coming next in life in our crossroads. This intersection is a place of being served and serving others.

Life overflows with waiting at different crossroads. Advent is a time of waiting, and we can learn a lesson about waiting with Elizabeth and Mary. We see how their crossroad moments flourished with blessings.

Waiting isn't empty time. Others wait with us at their own crossroads. We wait together in this active time of giving and receiving.

Waiting teaches us to bless, to become, to behold God and be loved by him.

Roadside Billboard

What we are waiting for is not as important as what happens to us while we are waiting.
Trust the process.

Mandy Hale

Roadside Pursuit

Think about others when you are in a time of waiting: don't focus so much on yourself, look around. Whom could you bless? What does the story of Elizabeth and Mary teach you? What are some lessons you have learned while waiting?

Roadside Rest Stop

Gracious Lord, you bless me in so many ways. Open my eyes to discover the gifts you bestow along my journey. Help me to take my eyes off my own journey to bless others along the way. Thank you for your blessings, and may I be a blessing to others.

Kindness Along the Way

Joseph went from the Galilean town of Nazareth up to Bethlehem in Judah, David's town, for the census. As a descendant of David, he had to go there. He went with Mary, his fiancée, who was pregnant. While they were there, the time came for her to give birth. She gave birth to a son, her firstborn. She wrapped him in a blanket and laid him in a manger, because there was no room in the hostel.
Luke 2: 4-7 The Message

I watched my hubby's hands clutch the steering wheel as we inched along the icy highway. All we wanted was to get home safe, but an unexpected blizzard blowing off the lake pelleted us with blinding snow. We prayed that we would stay on solid ground as we couldn't see the road clearly.

My fear mounted like the number of cars I saw in the ditch. I wasn't sure what was louder – the music from the radio, or my heart, which was pounding loudly and full of fear.

Finally, we saw the exit sign with two hotels near the road. We decided it was time to find refuge and drove into their joint, barely visible driveway. Tumbling into one of the hotel lobbies, we looked like two Eskimos after a long hunt in a storm.

But the news wasn't good.

No rooms at either hotel were available.

The young hotel clerk, overworked since his relief couldn't make it in due to the storm, smiled sympathetically and invited us to stay in the lobby. He provided two blankets and pillows, made us coffee, and showed us a nearby small bathroom.

We didn't sleep well in the rigid chairs, but were safe and warm. Grateful to see the sun and the skies clear the next morning, we finally headed home, thanking the clerk for his hospitality. He couldn't provide a room, but he provided what we needed.

There was no room at the inn for Mary and Joseph either. The Bible doesn't tell us if there was an innkeeper, but for many years children's pageants have personified this character who offers the stable for the son of God to be born. Our imaginations see this person as hospitable, empathetic, but on a whole, invisible.

A minor character along Mary and Joseph's path. One small link in the journey of Christ.

Along our way, we too meet people in passing. We offer a smile. We may say a short, affirming comment. Maybe we offer insignificant assistance. The simple act of that hotel clerk to find us pillows, offer us coffee, and give us a safe place to rest eased our discomfort. We never forgot his kindness.

We can be an innkeeper for others. We can intentionally seek opportunities to offer small gifts of time, kindness, and thinking of others – not just at Christmas, but throughout the year.

When I think about that stormy trip home, I smile as I remember the hospitality of one person who made us feel safe and "home." We too can do this for other people in our stormy journey in life.

Roadside Billboard

Remember there's no such thing as a small act of kindness. Every act creates a ripple with no logical end.
Scott Adams

Roadside Pursuit

Pay attention to where you can be kind today. Remember the times when simple acts of kindness and the thoughtfulness of others brightened your way.

Roadside Rest Stop

You are the Lord of all Kindness. Help me spread your love, grace, and mercy to others I meet along my journey.

Billboards and Flashing Road Signs

And there were shepherds living out in the fields nearby, keeping watch over their flocks at night. An angel of the Lord appeared to them, and the glory of the Lord shone around them, and they were terrified.

But the angel said to them, "Do not be afraid. I bring you good news that will cause great joy for all the people. Today in the town of David a Savior has been born to you; he is the Messiah, the Lord. This will be a sign to you: You will find a baby wrapped in cloths and lying in a manger."

Suddenly a great company of the heavenly host appeared with the angel, praising God and saying, "Glory to God in the highest heaven, and on earth peace to those on whom his favor rests."

When the angels had left them and gone into heaven, the shepherds said to one another, "Let's go to Bethlehem and see this thing that has happened, which the Lord has told us about."
Luke 2: 8-15

Bright yellow signs flash messages along our paths. Blinking words across a screen warn us about the upcoming detour, lane restrictions, and construction. A roadside notification may also tell us we are approaching an accident, an area known for fog or falling rocks, or even an "Amber Alert" for a missing child.

Billboards shout and tempt us to stop and buy, buy, buy. Some signs bring smiles to our faces with their humor such as "Buckle Up the Next Million Miles" or "Two Hour Parking between 7 and 8 pm."

Along the way, we find surprises and places to visit that we never had any intention of stopping to see. An unexpected find such as an out-of-the-way museum or historic place. On one trip, we read the billboard announcing we were near the location where "Field of Dreams" was filmed. We stopped and ran the bases on that ballfield.

As we travel and stop at unexpected places, we see the world with refreshing perspectives. This new outlook transforms our lives and our imaginations and opens us toward new directions.

One routine, mundane work night, angels surprised a group of shepherds outside of Bethlehem. The Good News arrived unannounced, unexpected, and out of the ordinary. A dazzling, powerful message transformed their lives forever.

God creates for us billboards with powerful messages of hope along our way. Pay attention to what you see along the journey. Be mindful of the blessings, opportunities, and unexpected insights. These oases refresh the soul and give us a foretaste of heaven to come.

God shows us the way, brings us joy, and nurtures us along our journeys by the sight, sounds, and experiences that cross our paths, especially at crossroads.

Divine billboards invite us to stop and discover unexpected delights. Be thankful and cherish the unexpected joys along your way.

Roadside Billboard

In moments of surprise we catch at least a glimpse of the joy to which gratefulness opens the door.
David Steindl-Rast

Roadside Pursuit

Make a list of divine billboards you have seen in the past, especially at crossroads. How does remembering those stops open your eyes to see more of God's gifts along the way?

Roadside Rest Stop

Giving God, thank you for making yourself known in my journey of life. Open my eyes to see where you are inviting me to stop, learn,

and be shaped by your hands to be the person you want me to be.
Thank you for the divine billboards.

Different Routes to Home

And having been warned in a dream not to go back to Herod, they (the Wise men) returned to their country by another route.
Matthew 2: 12

Life usually doesn't turn out how we imagine. The fairytale romance comes with difficulties, and even divorce. The perfect career plan takes longer and comes with more stress than planned. Parenting leads to sleeplessness, worry, and doubts.

Even after the kids leave and you enjoy the freedom of an empty nest, you still worry about them and have even less control over their circumstances. You want the family to be home at the holidays, but you smile with relief when they all leave and routines returns.

Our ideas about home evolve, mutate, and pivot by season, circumstance, and purpose.

What is home? Home can be a physical setting, such as your house, hometown, community, school or work. Home is where memories accumulate and shape our lives.

The emotional side of home appears in our desire to be loved, accepted and part of a family. The sense of belonging looms strong for our human nature.

In our minds, home is where we feel safe and comfortable.

For our spirit, home is with God.

Whenever we travel, when we turn toward home or arrive in the driveway, a wave of peace descends upon our souls. We are home.

The Wise Men were ready to take the long journey home. They found and worshiped the newborn King where the start had led them. They accomplished what they needed to do and started out on the road home.

But God told them in their dreams to take a different route home. They would still arrive back to the place they wanted to be, but through a longer and possibly more treacherous path home.

Home is the destination we seek all our lives. A place of full acceptance wrapped in love. We may not feel that way where we live now. We may be on a different route currently, but we head homeward throughout our lives.

Heaven is our home.

During Christmas, a hunger deepens within us. In this season full of nostalgia, sights and smells can bring back warm memories, along with emotionally charged family interactions.

Knowing God calls us homeward helps us to name this desire for home. Worship, prayer, and time with God determine the best route and bring joy to our time as we travel.

I wonder how the wise men were different after their journey. They experienced long, difficult travel, they talked with King Herod, and they had vivid dreams full of warnings. Then they spent time in the presence of the Messiah. This journey transformed them in surprising ways.

We are all heading home. We travel from and in different directions but with the same destination – home.

Roadside Billboard

At Christmas, all roads lead home.
Marjorie Holmes

Roadside Pursuit

What characteristics would you use to describe home? How has your image of home changed over the years? How is heaven a home for you? How does the Christmas season stir up your desire for home?

Roadside Rest Stop

Thank you, Lord, for creating a home for me. A temporary place of joy, growth, and love here on earth – and a final, magnificent dwelling with you forever.

Coming Home

When Joseph and Mary had done everything required by the Law of the Lord, they returned to Galilee to their own town of Nazareth. And the child grew and became strong; he was filled with wisdom, and the grace of God was on him. Luke 2: 39-40

In these verses, Mary and Joseph take Jesus, as required by the law, to Jerusalem to be consecrated to God. They walked the road to the big city and while in Jerusalem they happened to meet Simeon and Anna. It was a chance encounter that offered blessing and strength for their trip home.

What people along the way offer us wisdom and guidance? God continues to teach and form us not just while traveling to exotic places, but often in our own backyards.

Holidays often involve visits to hometowns, seeing childhood friends, and reconnecting with cousins, aunts, and uncles. We may be blessed with an insightful conversation with an old neighbor. We experience hope and joy when we open a Christmas card from a faraway friend. We allow our hearts to touch the ground beneath us for a moment of nostalgia and stability.

All nourishment for our journey of coming home.

What can our journeys teach us about home and discernment at the crossroads we encounter?

Home offers us a place where we grow in wisdom and grace, like the young Jesus did. Home grounds us. Home serves as shelter for facing our challenges. We pause in our homes to reflect on the season, family, friendships, and life.

Hopefully home gives us a sense of acceptance and love. We feel safe enough to openly express our ups and downs. We have room to stretch and grow. Home is a space where God shapes us with his grace.

During Christmas, take a moment to savor your home. Listen to its lessons before you continue on your journey. What is home telling you about your desires, compassion, and love, and how you want to live? What is God inviting you to learn from being home?

Come home this Christmas and spend time with God.

Roadside Billboard

A man travels the world over in search of what he needs and returns home to find it.
George Moore

Roadside Pursuit

What wisdom about being home do you need to take along on your journey? How does your past help you in the crossroads ahead?

Roadside Rest Stop

Lord of all Wisdom, help me see the lessons you have for me at home this Christmas so I may bring glory to you in all my actions and steps in life.

Jesus Walks with Us

They asked each other, "Were not our hearts burning within us while he talked with us on the road and opened the Scriptures to us?"
Luke 24: 32

Who walks with you on your journey? What companions share your discussions about the crossroads you come across?

The word "companion" means one who accompanies or associates with another. The word comes from Latin – com as in with and together, and panis as in bread. A companion is someone we share bread with on our journey.

The image of having a meal together, enjoying and taking in nourishment with another, is powerful. As we walk alongside each other and share our lives, the bread becomes the mingling of our conversations. We grow closer to others by listening, laughing, and telling stories. We take off our masks and feel safe to be vulnerable with intimate peeks into our hearts and souls.

Even in the times we feel alone, we have a Companion accompanying us. One who listens, One who walks with us. One who pauses when we stop at the crossroads and helps discern our next step.

Other companions emerge too. Lifelong friends. Seasonal acquaintance. Loved ones who want and need us too. People you meet once or twice and share a mutual experience.

On the road to the town called Emmaus, two friends walked. They shared their grief and fears, and they were surprised at the events that happened in Jerusalem. They heard that Jesus was crucified – the one they believed was the Messiah. But now they were confused by rumors that he didn't die. People told others they saw the risen Lord.

It was all too much to take in. Incomprehensible. Being overwhelmed, they go for a walk with a friend, hoping the time away will help them sort the confusion.

Another companion joins them. Jesus listens, asks questions, and points them to the scriptures. He shares bread with them. Not just the kind of bread we eat, but the kind of bread that feeds us spiritually.

The two walking to Emmaus felt their hearts burn, knowing Jesus accompanied them. We too know this Companion who walks alongside us on our roads. Jesus.

Roadside Billboard

I find Jesus my confidant and companion, brother, and savior; our relationship is intimate, vulnerable, demanding yet comfortable and reassuring.
Malcolm Boyd

Roadside Pursuit

Who accompanies you along the way? Ask God to send you partners to walk alongside you. Listen to their wisdom and share their joys. Express your appreciation to companions for their friendship and love.

Roadside Rest Stop

Thank you, Lord, for friends and family who accompany me on this journey through life. I ask you for just the right person to come alongside of me as I need them for companionship and camaraderie.

Crossroad Seasons

And this is my prayer: that your love may abound more and more in knowledge and depth of insight, so that you may be able to discern what is best and may be pure and blameless for the day of Christ, filled with the fruit of righteousness that comes through Jesus Christ – to the glory and praise of God.
Philippians 1: 9-11

Christmas season. Seasons of transitions. Growing seasons. Seasons of life.

We experience many seasons in our journey. Times of smooth, enjoyable scenery, and adventure, and difficult, rough moments when you don't know which way to turn.

No matter what season you are in – new job, parenthood, retirement, health crisis, church season, holiday season – you will come to intersections where discernment is necessary.

The spiritual practice of discernment is required when we enter the crossroads of life. Do we pause? Do we rest? Turn back? Start in a new direction? How do we hear God in these moments of confusion, indecision, and multiple options?

When we find ourselves at a crossroad, the best place to start is in prayer. Today's Bible verse offers us a framework to find words for our conversation with God.

Lord this is my prayer. I am at a crossroad and need your direction. I seek to know you more. To love you completely. To embrace your wisdom and insight so I know how to discern what is best in this gift of life from you.
Thank you for Jesus and I praise your holy name.
Amen.

We focus on love. We ask for knowledge and insight.

Next, we weigh the options. We seek what is pure, or the right action to take, even if inconvenient. What would Jesus do? What would yield fruit or best consequences? Pausing and listening to our heart and the voice of God, he slowly nudges us with his gentle whispers. Listen deeply and in silence for his direction.

Watch for the Holy Spirit, who will leave the fragrance of fruit around our decisions. Consider the choices producing joy, faith, gentleness, kindness, love, patience, and peace.

Be honest with yourself. Is this decision based more on ego or God? What would bring the most glory and honor to God?

Would going forward in this direction draw you closer to God? Or would it take away from experiencing God?

Every season gives us fresh growth when nourished by God's grace and love. When clarified through God first, our next step surfaces. Distilling a decision in the waters of God's compassion and guidance, the next step appears at every crossroad.

Roadside Billboard

True discernment means not only distinguishing the right from the wrong; it means distinguishing the primary from the secondary, the essential from the indifferent, and the permanent from the transient. And, yes, it means distinguishing between the good and the better, and even between the better and the best.
Sinclair B. Ferguson

Roadside Pursuit

Think about your process of making decisions. Do you start with God? Rewrite the Bible verse from today into your prayer for discernment.

Roadside Rest Stop

Lord, I start with you. I need help in this season of life, knowing which way to go. My heart wants to do only the activities that glorify you. Forgive my ego, fears, and self-esteem for taking over, especially in this busy season of Christmas. Grant me peace, goodness, and faith on each step of this journey we are taking together.

Crossroads with Jesus

In the beginning was the Word, and the Word was with God, and the Word was God.
He was with God in the beginning.
Through him all things were made; without him nothing was made that has been made.
In him was life, and that life was the light of all mankind. The light shines in the darkness,
and the darkness has not overcome it.
John 1: 1

Holidays bring out the whole gamut of emotions. Joy in being with friends and family. Anger and disappointment in stressed encounters in crowded stores. Hearts full of demanding expectations. Even our friends and family contribute to seasonal stress.

One of the largest emotions to surface during Christmas season is loneliness. Feelings of isolation also arise at other holidays, such as Mother's Day, birthdays and significant anniversaries.

When facing decisions at crossroads in life, we may feel alone. Loneliness feeds our self-pity, which in turn takes us further away from others. We tell ourselves no one asks, invites, or includes us. We withdraw into a barren heart, empty and drained psychology and spiritually.

Elizabeth Elliot wrote, "Loneliness is a wilderness, but through receiving it as a gift, accepting it from the hand of God, and offering it back to him with thanksgiving, it may become a pathway to holiness, to glory and to God himself."

Could our negative emotions be a present this season? Naming what is going on in our spirit is the beginning of unwrapping a beautiful gift. Loneliness may open the door of our hearts to recognize our fellow human pilgrims accompanying us.

Jesus too walks along our side in our loneliness and indecisions.

Jesu was present at the beginning of all life, of our life. In him is life, your life. With him is the light, even in our darkest times.

We are not alone. God is with us at all our crossroads.

Dag Hammarskjöld wrote with wisdom about the negative side of emotions, keeping us awake at night and feeling empty within our hearts. "Pray that your loneliness," he said, "may spur you into finding something to live for, great enough to die for."

Loneliness may be one of your best gifts this year. You will find God with you in every emotion, moment, and crossroad.

We are not alone.

Roadside Billboard

The next time you find yourself alone in a dark alley facing the undeniables of life, don't cover them with a blanket, or ignore them with a nervous grin. Don't turn up the TV and pretend they aren't there. Instead, stand still, whisper his name, and listen. He is nearer than you think.
Max Lucado

Roadside Pursuit

Name what is stirring within you. List every emotion in your journal. Talk with God about these feelings and ask him to show you the lessons to learn at this crossroad you face. Thank God for being with you every step of the way.

Roadside Rest Stop

Thank you, Lord, for your help, wisdom, and guidance when I get so full of mixed up, confusing emotions. I stumble at this crossroads but know you pick me up. Guide me. Stay with me. Show me the gifts you have for me at this time and place of my life.

Our only desire and our one choice should be this:

*I want and I choose
what better leads to
God's deepening life in me.*

St. Ignatius Loyola

A Christmas Prayer and Blessing

May the seasons of your life bring fresh growth and new adventures.

May Christmas brim with laughter and love.

May the joy and peace of seasonal lights bring brightness to your crossroads.

May your heart be singled focused on God and you feel his touch along your way.

May your mind be open to new ideas and delightful thoughts.

May your spirit be lifted up by our time in Advent and strengthen to face exciting new days.

May God be the center and the catalyst of all your choices – great and small.

Jean Wise

Author Notes

- Explore spiritual blogs, full of new approaches and fellow companions on this faith walk. I invite you to come to my blog: healthyspirituality.org

- You also may be interested in the books I write to help you along the way: Whispers, Being with God in Breath Prayers, Spiritual Retreats, a Guide to Slowing Down to be with God, and 40 Voices, A Lenten Devotional. See all my books and new releases at healthyspirituality.org/amazon

- I am always adding more resources and ideas on the blog, healthyspirituality.org. Please subscribe so you don't miss out!

- Did you find this book helpful? Please take a minute to leave an honest review on Amazon. It is a wonderful way to say thank you to an author.

- Interested in going deeper?
Prayer Journaling Course: A Practical Guide to Organize, Prioritize and Energize your Conversations with God. Order the course now for only $12 by going to: https://www.gumroad.com/products/CqGK

Let's connect and share our journeys together –

My author's Facebook page, https://www.facebook.com/Jeanwiseauthor

Twitter https://twitter.com/Jeanwise

Pinterest https://www.pinterest.com/jeanwise22

About the Author

Jean Wise is a writer, speaker, retreat leader, and spiritual director. She is a contributor author of devotions for four compilations, as well as the author of several books.

She has also written numerous devotionals, magazine articles, and newspaper features. You can find her books at healthyspirituality.org/amazon.

Jean is a Deacon at St. Peter's Lutheran Church facilitating adult spiritual formation. She has an
active spiritual direction practice including leading group spiritual direction. She is a frequent speaker for gathering and retreats in northwest Ohio.

An RN with her Masters in Nursing, Jean retired from public health in 2006 as the County Health Commissioner to focus on freelance speaking and writing. She discovered her calling to nurture others, as she practiced in nursing, and now as she helps others grow closer to God in her ministry of spiritual direction, writing, and speaking.

Don't Forget to Get the Bonus! Enter your email at http://healthyspirituality.org/advent to receive the Advent Resource Guide.

Blessings!

www.ingramcontent.com/pod-product-compliance
Lightning Source LLC
Chambersburg PA
CBHW061340040426
42444CB00011B/3013